THE AMISTAD MUTINY

"Dear friend Mr. Adams.
We love you very much. . . .
We ask, we beg you to tell court
let Mendi people be free."

~ KIN-NA ~

IN A LETTER TO JOHN QUINCY ADAMS
WRITTEN ON THE EVE OF THE
AMISTAD TRIAL

BY BARBARA A. SOMERVILL

Published by The Child's World®
1980 Lookout Drive, Mankato, MN 56003-1705
800-599-READ • www.childsworld.com

CONTENT CONSULTANT

Joanna Banks, Museum Educator
Washington, DC

PHOTOS

Cover and page 4: Picture History/Newscom
Interior: AP Photo: 14, 29; AP Photo/Nazia Parvez: 12; AP Photo/Talladega
Daily Home: 22; Everett Collection/Shutterstock.com: 9, 19; Library of Congress,
Prints and Photographs Division: 10, 16, 18, 31; The Miriam and Ira D. Wallach
Division of Art, Prints, and Photographs/The New York Public Library: 17;
Morphart Creation/Shutterstock.com: 23, 28 (right); National Portrait Gallery,
Smithsonian Institution, Frederick Hill Meserve Collection: 21; National Portrait
Gallery, Smithsonian Institution, Gift from the Trustees of the Corcoran Gallery
of Art: 20; National Portrait Gallery, Smithsonian Institution: 24; North Wind
Picture Archives: 5, 6, 7, 8, 27, 28 (left); Schomburg Center for Research in Black
Culture, Jean Blackwell Hutson Research and Reference Division, The New
York Public Library: 11; US National Archives and Records Administration: 25

LIBRARY OF CONGRESS CATALOGING-IN-PUBLICATION DATA

ISBN 9781503853706 (Reinforced Library Binding)
ISBN 9781503854062 (Portable Document Format)
ISBN 9781503854185 (Online Multi-user eBook)
LCCN: 2020943351

Printed in the United States of America

Cover and page 4 caption:
The *Amistad* as it
looked in 1840.

CONTENTS

Chapter One

THE SALE OF HUMAN BEINGS

In 1492, Christopher Columbus landed on an island in the Caribbean Sea and, although **indigenous** people were already living there, claimed it for Spain. Other European explorers arrived after Columbus. They claimed land in the Americas for and, France, Portugal, and the Netherlands. European kings and queens gave away land in the Americas to friends and relatives.

The European landowners wanted to make money from their land. They built large farms, or plantations, to grow cotton, tobacco, sugar, coffee, and **indigo**. But the landowners needed many people to handle all of these crops. The need for workers created a thriving industry—the sale of human beings.

Columbus landing on the island of San Salvador in the Bahamas in 1492.

Estimates suggest that from the early 1500s to the late 1870s, more than 9 million people from Africa were shipped to the Americas. Millions died on the journey. The slave traders packed as many Africans in their ships' **holds** as possible. The captive Africans had to survive hunger, thirst, filth, and whippings. At slave markets, land-owners inspected, bought, and sold Africans like furniture. After being bought, the enslaved people lived and worked in conditions that were often just as horrible.

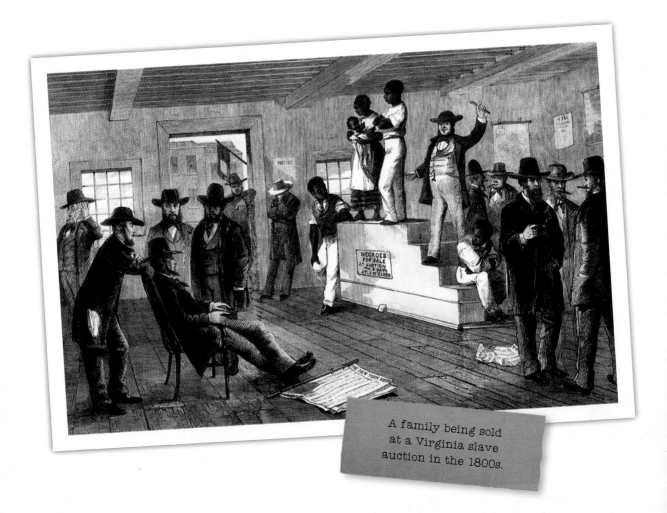

A family being sold at a Virginia slave auction in the 1800s.

In the early 1800s, **abolitionists** spoke out against slavery in the United States. Several northern states stopped traders from bringing newly enslaved people to their shores. Some states banned slavery altogether. Yet, slavery continued to expand in the southern United States, as well as Brazil and Cuba. The slave traders, who were making a lot of money, kept shipping Africans to sell into slavery. The sale of human beings was a profitable industry. The *Amistad* was one of the ships involved in this business.

A number of the United States' Founding Fathers and early presidents enslaved people. George Washington, Thomas Jefferson, James Madison, Benjamin Franklin, and Patrick Henry are just a few examples.

Captured Africans were marched to the coast where they would be sold as slaves and loaded onto ships.

Chapter Two

THE DARK JOURNEY

The story of the *Amistad* begins in Africa. A man named Sengbe Pieh (SENG-bay PEE-yeh) was a farmer and Mende (or Mendi) tribal leader in a village in present-day Sierra Leone. In April 1839, Sengbe Pieh was tending his crops when Africans from another tribe captured him. The men sold Sengbe Pieh to a slave factory on the Gallinas River.

The slave factory was a huge, open-air prison that housed hundreds of men, women, and children. They had no protection from the sun or rain. Most of the captives, in their 20s, were strong and healthy. They needed their strength to survive what awaited them.

Captives such as Sengbe Pieh were sometimes tied to logs or trees until they were sold.

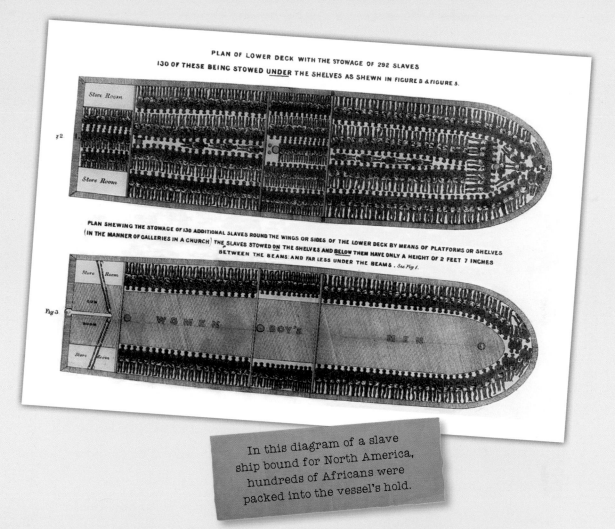

PLAN OF LOWER DECK WITH THE STOWAGE OF 292 SLAVES
130 OF THESE BEING STOWED <u>UNDER</u> THE SHELVES AS SHEWN IN FIGURE D & FIGURE S.

PLAN SHEWING THE STOWAGE OF 130 ADDITIONAL SLAVES ROUND THE WINGS OR SIDES OF THE LOWER DECK BY MEANS OF PLATFORMS OR SHELVES (IN THE MANNER OF GALLERIES IN A CHURCH) THE SLAVES STOWED <u>ON</u> THE SHELVES AND <u>BELOW</u> THEM HAVE ONLY A HEIGHT OF 2 FEET 7 INCHES BETWEEN THE BEAMS: AND FAR LESS UNDER THE BEAMS. See Fig 1.

In this diagram of a slave ship bound for North America, hundreds of Africans were packed into the vessel's hold.

That spring, the Portuguese ship *Tecora* anchored near the slave factory. The ship's captain bought more than 500 people, including Sengbe Pieh. The Africans were loaded aboard the *Tecora*, which was bound for Havana, Cuba. Crewmen stripped the Africans of their clothes and chained them together in twos. The slave traders stuffed the Africans onto shallow decks in the ship's hold. Barely 4 feet (1.2 meters) separated one rack of humans from the next. The traders packed the Africans like sardines in a can. The more enslaved people they delivered to Cuba, the more money they would make.

During the trip to Cuba, the Africans received very little water and some rice. Those who did not eat were beaten. Some ate until they vomited. Most of the time, the Africans lay on wooden racks, unable even to turn over. Because the hold had no bathrooms, they lay in their own body waste.

An 1840 illustration of Sengbe Pieh.

For two months, Sengbe Pieh and the other Africans suffered from seasickness, thirst, and hunger. Many Africans died on the trip. A slave trader usually lost about one-third of the ship's human cargo—about 160 people. Those who survived arrived at the port filthy, thin, and sickly.

Finally, the *Tecora* anchored off Havana, Cuba, in June 1839.

The slave traders unloaded their human cargo late at night. Although bringing new enslaved people into Cuba was against Spanish law, the traders were able to get around the rules by calling the slaves *ladinos*, or people born into slavery in Cuba before 1820.

Then the enslaved people were cleaned, dressed, and fed. The traders wanted the slaves to look as healthy as possible so they would fetch a top price. The slaves crowded into large prisons called **barracoons** until they were sold at the slave market.

Two Spaniards named Pedro Montes and José Ruiz bought enslaved people from the *Tecora*. Montes chose four children. Ruiz selected 49 adults, including Sengbe Pieh. He paid $450 for each person. The two men also bought false papers stating their slaves were Cuban-born *ladinos* and changed the slaves' names. Sengbe Pieh was given the Spanish name Joseph Cinque. (SING-kay).

On June 28, 1839, Montes and Ruiz loaded their 53 Mende slaves onto a **schooner** called the *Amistad*. They worked in darkness to avoid Spanish inspectors. The word *amistad* means "friendship" in Spanish, but there was nothing friendly about life on this vessel. The ship's crew treated the enslaved people like animals. Men had iron **shackles** around their ankles. Rough **manacles** cut their wrists. Metal collars linked one person to another. The women and children were tied together with rope.

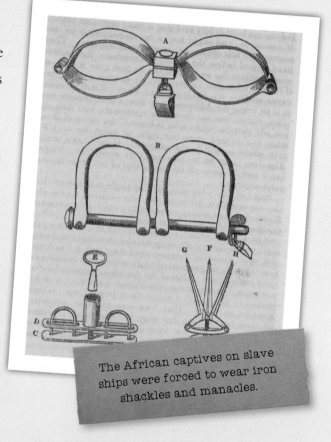

The African captives on slave ships were forced to wear iron shackles and manacles.

Again, the Africans were forced below the main deck into a dark, airless hold. The *Amistad's* hold was so shallow that the Africans sat crouched together, one behind the other. There was no room to stand.

The captain of the *Amistad*, Ramón Ferrer, took pride in his speedy black schooner. Built in Baltimore, Maryland, the ship was sleek and easy to handle. Ferrer's crew included a Black cabin boy named Antonio, a cook named Celestino, and two crew members.

Ruiz and Montes owned the ship's extensive cargo. It included jewelry, dishes, silverware, cloth, other household goods, leather, gear for horses, and knives for cutting sugarcane.

A normal trip to the Cuban port of Guanaja took about three days. This time, storms struck the Caribbean Sea, and the *Amistad* drifted off course. The Africans, huddled in the hold, feared for their lives.

On the third day, Captain Ferrer realized the trip would take several more days. He cut the food and water rations for the enslaved people. A day's food for each person was a banana, two potatoes, and a cup of water. When one of the Africans tried to take more water, a member of the crew whipped him.

The *Amistad*, shown here as a modern-day reconstruction, had two masts and a narrow hull.

Then, the *Amistad's* cook played a cruel joke on the enslaved people. Through hand signals, he told the Africans that the crew was going to kill and eat them. In the six months since his capture, Sengbe Pieh had seen his people jailed, starved, chained, and beaten. He had seen dead Africans tossed overboard like trash. Why would he not believe this frightening story? Sengbe Pieh talked with his fellow captives, and they came up with a plan.

Chapter Three

MUTINY ON THE *AMISTAD*

On deck during mealtime, Sengbe Pieh found a loose nail and pried it free. Later that night, he used the nail to unlock his shackles. He freed his fellow captives from their chains. The men searched the cargo for weapons and found the knives and some heavy sticks.

At around 4 A.M., on July 1, 1839, thick clouds covered the moon and stars. The captives were ready. In the darkness, Sengbe Pieh and two other captives named Grabeau and Burnah led the **mutiny**. The Africans poured onto the deck armed with knives and sticks.

The freed captives slashed at the captain and his crew. Sengbe Pieh struck Captain Ferrer with his knife. Ferrer dropped to the deck, and other captives strangled him.

Pedro Montes drew a knife and tried to drive the Africans back into the hold. The captives did not retreat. They surged forward and hit Montes with knives, sticks, and oars. José Ruiz fought hard, but the Africans overpowered him, too.

In a short time, the Mendian captives took charge of the ship. Captain Ferrer and the cook Celestino lay dead. The ship's two crewmen jumped overboard and probably drowned. The Africans lashed the cabin boy, Antonio, to the anchor but did not hurt him. Ruiz surrendered and begged that his life be spared. Montes suffered deep gashes during the short battle. He crept into the hold to hide behind some food barrels. When the freed captives found him, Montes, too, begged Sengbe Pieh for his life.

This illustration shows the mutiny on the *Amistad*.

Sengbe Pieh and his fellow Africans now faced a serious problem. No one in the group knew anything about sailing a ship like the *Amistad*. They decided to spare Ruiz and Montes and ordered them to sail toward the rising sun in the East—toward Africa.

This plan seemed sensible since the *Tecora* had sailed toward the setting sun during their trip across the Atlantic Ocean. However, the Africans could not tell direction by the night sky. Ruiz and Montes used the former captives' lack of knowledge to trick them.

Ruiz and Montes sailed eastward during the day, as they were ordered. To slow the trip east, Montes allowed the sails to flap in the breeze. At night, however, the Spaniards let the sails fill with wind. They changed direction and headed northwest. They hoped to find another ship to save them.

The *Amistad* traveled a strange, zigzagging course up the East Coast of the United States. Several ships spotted the *Amistad* on its odd journey. When the ships' captains saw armed Africans on the deck, they left the *Amistad* alone.

Food and water were in short supply. The original plan was to spend three or four days—not two months—at sea. The ship wandered along its course through July and into August. By this time, the Africans were faring poorly. Many became sick and died. Finding a port to buy supplies became urgent.

On August 25, 1839, the *Amistad* anchored off Culloden Point at the eastern end of Long Island in New York. Sengbe Pieh and several of the men rowed ashore to buy food, water, and supplies. They used Spanish gold to pay for whatever they wanted.

Near where the *Amistad* had anchored, the USS *Washington*, a survey ship, was mapping the shoreline. While on duty, Lieutenant Richard Meade spotted the Africans onshore. The ship's captain, Lieutenant Thomas R. Gedney, ordered Meade to investigate. The next day, Meade and a small crew boarded and took control of the *Amistad*.

Gedney estimated the captives to be worth between $20,000 and $30,000, which was a small fortune then. (In 1839, the U.S. president's yearly salary was $25,000.) Gedney and his crew hoped to claim the *Amistad* and its cargo—including the captives—as **salvage**.

It was Lieutenant Richard Meade who first noticed the *Amistad* Africans on U.S. land.

Chapter Four

DECISIONS AND DISAGREEMENTS

Now Lieutenant Thomas R. Gedney had to make a decision. Should he take the *Amistad* captives to a New York harbor or to Connecticut? Since New York had banned slavery, the *Amistad* Africans would not be considered property there. Connecticut still allowed slavery, however. There he could claim the ship and everything on it under salvage laws. With money in mind, Gedney ordered Meade to take the *Amistad* to New London, Connecticut.

After the *Amistad* and the USS *Washington* arrived in New London, Gedney sent a message to U.S. officials in New Haven, Connecticut. He and the USS *Washington's* crew had claimed the *Amistad*, its goods, and the Africans as salvage.

This 1852 illustration shows New London's busy harbor.

This portrait was completed while Sengbe Pieh awaited trial.

On August 29, 1839, Judge Andrew T. Judson held a hearing. He listened to Gedney's claims as well as Ruiz and Montes's story. Ruiz and Montes wanted the *Amistad* and all its cargo—including captives— returned to them. Judson ruled that the Africans on the *Amistad* should be charged with mutiny and murder. Sengbe Pieh, the remaining 38 adult Africans, the cabin boy Antonio, and the four Mendian children landed in jail.

Abolitionists, led by New Yorker Lewis Tappan, quickly arrived to support the African prisoners. Because the Mendians spoke no English, they couldn't explain what had happened. The abolitionists looked for someone to translate English and Mende. They eventually found a man named James Covey, who helped the Africans tell their side of the story.

There were several issues to be decided in the *Amistad* case. The first issue was where the case should be tried. Should the trial be held in New York or Connecticut and in federal or state court? The ship had been captured in New York waters, but it was brought to Connecticut for salvage.

Lewis Tappan

The second issue was who had rights in the case. Who could legally claim the *Amistad* and its goods? Several people claimed those rights: some New Yorkers who sold supplies to Sengbe Pieh and his men, Lieutenant Gedney and the USS *Washington* crew, and finally, Ruiz and Montes.

The third issue was what the exact nature of the cargo was. Were the African captives property or human beings?

Many other issues arose before the *Amistad* trial started. The case caused national and international conflict. Within the United States, some people favored slavery and others opposed it. In the South, wealthy plantation owners who depended on slave labor wanted the *Amistad* Africans to be considered property. On the other side, abolitionists wanted the *Amistad* Africans set free. They believed that the Africans had a right to fight against being enslaved.

Outside of the United States, the government of Spain objected because the *Amistad* and its cargo had belonged to Spanish citizens. They wanted the ship and all its cargo—including the Africans—returned to Ruiz and Montes. The Spanish government pressured President Martin Van Buren to return the *Amistad*. It seemed, however, that the decision rested with the courts, not the president.

Van Buren expected trouble with politicians from the South and with the Spanish if the court ruled in favor of the captives. So, Van Buren ordered the skipper of a schooner docked in New Haven harbor, the USS *Grampus*, to take the Mendians to Cuba if that should be the decision of the court. All this happened before the trial had even started!

President Martin Van Buren wanted to return the *Amistad* Africans to Cuba.

Sengbe Pieh gave a somber, moving speech to the other Africans after the mutiny. He told them, "I am resolved it is better to die than to be a white man's slave."

Chapter Five

THE TRIAL

A number of famous—and not so famous—people were involved in the *Amistad* trial. It was not a jury trial. That meant a judge would decide the **verdict**. Again, the judge was Andrew T. Judson. **Attorney** William S. Holabird presented the government's case against the *Amistad* Africans. The lawyers defending the Africans included Roger S. Baldwin, Seth Staples, and Theodore Sedgwick. These men were famous lawyers in the 1830s.

Andrew Judson had earned a name for himself as someone who favored slavery. In 1833, as a state attorney in Connecticut, Judson had tried a woman named Prudence Crandall for running a school that taught African American girls in Canterbury, Connecticut. She was found guilty, but the decision was later reversed. A mob burned Crandall's school to the ground, however, and she left the state. The school never reopened. Judson had been a judge for four years when the *Amistad* trial came to his courtroom.

Roger S. Baldwin

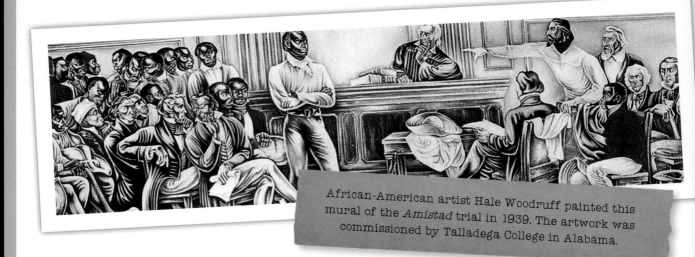

African-American artist Hale Woodruff painted this mural of the *Amistad* trial in 1939. The artwork was commissioned by Talladega College in Alabama.

William Holabird did not want the *Amistad* case to go to trial. He hoped President Van Buren would solve the problem for him by swift presidential action. However, Holabird clearly favored slavery.

In a letter to a fellow lawyer, he said, "I should regret extremely if the rascally blacks should fall into the hands of the abolitionists, with whom Hartford [Connecticut] is filled."

Abolitionists chose Roger Baldwin to lead the defense team. In 1831, Baldwin opposed an angry mob protesting the building of a training school for African Americans. His plan to defend the *Amistad* Africans included accusing Ruiz and Montes of being criminals.

After representing the *Amistad* Africans in court, Roger Baldwin went on to serve as the governor of Connecticut as well as a U.S. senator.

He hoped to prove that the Mendians should not be considered property because they were never truly slaves.

The trial began in September 1839. Sengbe Pieh and the other Mendians arrived in the courtroom. The defense lawyer called Sengbe Pieh to the witness stand. James Covey translated the Africans' story for the court.

Covey explained that the Mendians had been among 500 or more Africans taken to Cuba on the Portuguese ship *Tecora*. After being placed in a barracoon, they were sold to Ruiz and Montes. Then, they boarded the *Amistad*. The Africans told of the trip to Guanaja. They told about the cook's threat to kill and eat them and described their fight against their owners. The court heard about how the captives were chained and beaten, starved and denied water, then jailed.

The court also heard from Ruiz and Montes. They claimed that the Africans were *ladinos* and, therefore, legally enslaved. Ruiz and Montes presented their false papers.

Baldwin argued against the claim that the Africans were *ladinos*. He said, "Here are three children, between the ages of seven and nine years, who are proved to be native Africans....They were not born slaves, they were born in Africa." Baldwin pointed out that none of the Africans spoke Spanish, the language of Cuba. Finally, he argued that the Africans were not property but people.

This illustration shows slaves being shackled before being put in a ship's hold in 1830. The *Amistad* Africans described similar conditions to the court with the help of a translator.

On January 15, 1840, Judge Judson delivered his verdict. He said that Lieutenant Gedney and his crew could claim salvage of the *Amistad* and its cargo. But, he added, the Africans were not part of that cargo. Judson ruled that the cabin boy and slave Antonio should be returned to his owners in Cuba.

The most surprising thing Judson said was that the Africans were neither slaves nor Spanish subjects. They were free men and women. Judson added, "Cinque [Sengbe Pieh] and Grabeau shall not sigh for Africa in vain." Judson recommended that President Van Buren have a ship take the Africans home.

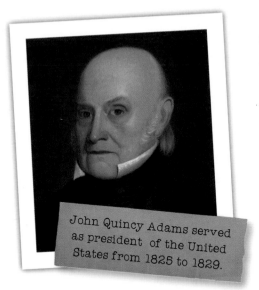

John Quincy Adams served as president of the United States from 1825 to 1829.

Although the abolitionists had won, they were still concerned that Van Buren would send the Africans back to Cuba to please the Spanish. To protect the Africans, the abolitionists took the case to the U.S. Supreme Court. Baldwin continued as the Africans' lawyer. The abolitionists also asked John Quincy Adams, former president of the United States, to speak for the Africans.

In the Supreme Court case, government lawyers argued that the papers for the *Amistad* were correct. Because the papers were in order, the Africans were slaves and property of Ruiz and Montes. These lawyers said that Spain demanded that the Africans be returned to Cuba, where they would be tried again for mutiny and murder.

Baldwin rose for the defense. He said that a U.S. court had already declared the Africans free people. As free people, he said, they had the right to fight against being enslaved.

Then John Quincy Adams spoke. He said that President Van Buren had no interest in justice. Adams said that right and wrong did not matter to Van Buren as long as the Spanish were happy with the result. Adams pointed out that the president had no say in matters of the courts, according to the laws set up in the U.S. Constitution.

The 1841 court decision written by Justice Joseph Story in the *Amistad* case.

Finally, the Supreme Court ruled. The judges said that the Africans had never been legally the property or slaves of Ruiz and Montes. They were not pirates, robbers, or murderers. They were free people who had been kidnapped from their homes.

The court turned the Africans over to a group called the *Amistad* Committee. The group worked to raise money to transport the Africans back to their homeland. Since the beginning of their dark journey, 18 of the Africans from the *Amistad* had died. It took many more months before the *Amistad* Committee could collect enough money to pay for the trip.

Chapter Six

A LEGACY OF FREEDOM

The *Amistad* trial increased awareness of the slavery issue in the United States. The abolitionists considered the verdicts in both courts to be victories against slavery. Those in favor of slavery said the verdicts did not affect enslaved people in the United States. Both sides were right.

The *Amistad* Africans were declared free people and not possessions. However, enslaved people within the United States were still considered property of their owners. In this regard, nothing had changed.

Spain continued to press the U.S. government about the *Amistad* verdicts. They wanted payment for the loss of the ship and its cargo, including the Africans. They never received a penny. They wanted the *Amistad* Africans returned to Cuba, which did not happen.

Antonio, the cabin boy who had been declared a slave, was supposed to be sent back to Cuba. Mysteriously, he disappeared. A year or so after the trial ended, Antonio reappeared in Canada. Abolitionists had helped him flee the United States to live in Montreal, Quebec.

Many people were outraged that President Van Buren had tried to force the courts to rule against the *Amistad* Africans. The *Hartford Courant* newspaper attacked Van Buren and his handling of the *Amistad* case. It wrote, "Surely Martin Van Buren is playing the part of a tyrant with a high hand—else why this tampering with our courts of justice."

People turned against Van Buren for trying to influence the courts. He was defeated in the next presidential election by William Henry Harrison.

As for the *Amistad* Africans, they finally made it back to Sierra Leone. On November 27, 1841, the remaining 35 Mendians and a group of **missionaries** boarded the *Gentleman* for the trip home. The journey took seven weeks. When they landed in Sierra Leone, Kin-na, one of the Mendians who had learned English, wrote to Lewis Tappan. He said, "We have reached Sierra Leone and one little while after we go to Mendi and we land very safely."

The missionaries who traveled with the *Amistad* Africans founded a Christian mission in Sierra Leone in 1842. Many of the Mendians stayed at the mission. Sengbe Pieh, however, chose to go home to his family. When he arrived, he found that his wife and children had died. He did not return to the mission until 1879. Old and sickly, Sengbe Pieh had returned to die.

African Americans celebrating freedom in 1866.

The *Amistad* captives were estimated to be worth $20,000–$30,000.
Can you put a price on a person's life? If so, what would you
consider when figuring out how much a person is worth?

**One of the main arguments for the defense in the *Amistad* case
was that the captive Africans were people.**
Can people be property? Is there a situation in which
it is okay to consider a person as property?

TIME LINE

1500s

European nations begin
shipping African captives to the
Americas to work as slaves.

1790

1799
New York passes a law
saying that all children born
to enslaved persons after
July 4, 1799, are to be freed
at age 28 for men and
age 25 for women.

1800-1820

Early 1800s
Abolitionists speak out against
slavery in the United States.

1817
Spain signs a treaty with Great
Britain, ending foreign slave
trade in all Spanish lands.

1820
Legal slave trade ends in Cuba.
Illegal trading of enslaved
people continues.

**How did President Martin Van Buren
use his power in the *Amistad* case?**
Do you think his actions were within his rights as a president?
Explain your answer.

1830

1837
Slave traders bring 25,000 Africans to Cuba. Many Africans die on the trip.

1839
Sengbe Pieh is captured from Sierra Leone. He sails on the *Tecora* bound for Havana, Cuba, to be sold into slavery. Now a slave, he is loaded onto the *Amistad* to sail to Guanaja, Cuba. On July 1, Sengbe Pieh helps lead a mutiny. In August, the *Amistad* is taken to New London, Connecticut, where the Africans are charged with mutiny and murder. In September, their trial begins.

1840

1840
Judge Andrew T. Judson rules that the Africans are to be turned over to U.S. president Martin Van Buren and returned to Africa.

1841
In February, the U.S. Supreme Court rules that the Africans were kidnapped and are free people. In November, the *Gentleman* sails to Sierra Leone with 35 surviving Mendians and a group of missionaries.

1842
The Christian missionaries who traveled with the *Amistad* Africans found the Mende Mission in Sierra Leone.

1870

1879
An old man, Sengbe Pieh returns to the Mende Mission to die.

**abolitionists
(AB-uh-LISH-uhn-ists)**
Abolitionists were people who worked against slavery in the 1800s in the United States. Abolitionists did not believe in the practice of owning human beings.

attorney (uh-TUR-nee)
An attorney is a lawyer. In the *Amistad* trial, the attorney who presented the government's case against the Africans was William Holabird.

barracoons (bar-uh-KOONZ)
Barracoons are large, plain buildings used as prisons. Captives in Cuba lived in barracoons until they were sold at the slave market.

holds (HOHLDZ)
Holds are the parts of ships where cargo is stored. Slave traders packed as many Africans in their ships' holds as possible.

indigenous (in-DIJ-uh-nuss)
Indigenous people are the first people to be living in a place. Columbus claimed areas for Spain, even though indigenous people were already living there.

indigo (IN-deh-goh)
Indigo is a plant with berries that can be used to make a purple-blue dye. Plantations in the South grew cotton, tobacco, sugar, coffee, and indigo.

manacles (MAA-nuh-kles)
Manacles are a type of handcuffs. The *Amistad* captives wore manacles that cut their wrists.

**missionaries
(MISH-uh-nayr-eez)**
Missionaries are people who travel to foreign lands to teach their faith and do other charitable works. The Mendians returned to Sierra Leone with a group of missionaries who hoped to bring Christianity to the people there.

mutiny (MYOOT-uh-nee)
A mutiny is an open rebellion against the people in charge, often on a ship. The *Amistad* captives Sengbe Pieh, Grabeau, and Burnah led a mutiny against the ship's captain and crew.

salvage (SAL-vij)
Salvage is payment for finding a lost ship, cargo, or both. Gedney and his men hoped to claim the *Amistad*, its cargo, and the slaves as salvage.

schooner (SKOO-nur)
A schooner is a fast-sailing ship with two masts. In 1839, Pedro Montes, José Ruiz, their crew, and their 53 Mende slaves left for the Americas on a schooner called the *Amistad*.

shackles (SHA-kles)
Shackles are chains on the legs or arms of a prisoner. The slave traders put iron shackles around Sengbe Pieh's ankles.

verdict (VUHR-dikt)
The verdict is the decision of the judge or jury in a trial. In the *Amistad* trial, Judge Andrew Judson delivered the verdict.

FURTHER INFORMATION

BOOKS

Alexander, Richard. *The Transatlantic Slave Trade: The Forced Migration of Africans to America.* New York, NY: PowerKids Press, 2016.

Asim, Jabari. *A Child's Introduction to African American History: The Experiences, People, and Events That Shaped Our Country.* New York, NY: Black Dog & Leventhal, 2018.

Baumann, Susan K. *The Middle Passage and the Revolt on the* Amistad. New York, NY: Rosen, 2013.

Edinger, Monica. *Africa Is My Home: A Child of the* Amistad. Somerville, MA Candlewick Press, 2015.

Nelson, Kadir. *Heart and Soul: The Story of America and African Americans.* Solon, OH: Findaway World, 2019.

WEBSITES

Visit our website for links about the *Amistad* mutiny:

childsworld.com/links

Note to Parents, Teachers, and Librarians: We routinely verify our Web links to make sure they are safe, active sites—so encourage your readers to check them out!

31

INDEX